Embrace Your "No"
5 Tips to Unlock Your Life and Find Peace

Dr. Katherine Y. Brown

www.TrueVinePublishing.org

Embrace Your No
Dr. Katherine Y. Brown

Published by True Vine Publishing Co.
810 Dominican Dr.
Nashville, TN 37228
www.TrueVinePublishing.org

ISBN: 978-1-962783-43-9 Paperback
ISBN 978-1-962783-39-2 eBook

Printed in the United States of America—First printing

Dedication

This book is dedicated to every individual who feels overwhelmed, stretched thin, and pulled in different directions. To the strong, the brave, and the selfless, the yes people of the world: may you discover through these pages the power of no, and learn to use it not as a barrier, but as a way to unlock your peace and, ultimately, make time to say yes to the things that truly serve you well. To those who have poured out their energy in service to others, often neglecting their own needs and desires: this book is for you. To those who feel obligated to say yes at the expense of their own peace and happiness: it's time to unlearn negative habits and relearn something new that benefits you. May your journey of self-discovery and self-love begin today. Finally, I dedicate this book to my loved ones, who have been my source of inspiration and strength and who have taught me the impact of both yes and no.

Sincerely,
Katherine

Table of Contents

Preface

It's time to pause and put yourself first. No matter where you find yourself in life, peace and balance can often be found by the articulation of two letters that form the word no. Through this book, I am inviting you to learn to utilize this powerful word with intention. The word no can be a complete sentence, and you own when to use this word in your daily life.

Are you someone who has oftentimes found yourself seeking validation and always saying yes? You are not alone. For the greater part of my existence, the word yes was something that I used as if it were the key to fulfillment, capable of resolving everything. My initial goal was to always be a strong supporter for everyone else. I consistently supported others but rarely took time for my own well-being. My yes to others became a barrier to my attaining my own personal goals. In some instances, I minimized my self-worth by ignoring my own needs to focus on the needs of others. While intentions to help, empower, and show compassion to others resulted in positive outcomes for them, it was often to my own detriment and with much sacrifice. In some ways, I think I was trained by society to believe that self-sacrifice and service to others should often take precedence over everything else, even if everything else was me. I have since learned to master the word no. Guess what? You can also. In fact, once you begin to practice using the word no, you can determine when you need to embrace your no because it can be as powerful as your yes.

Author's Note:

This book is about lifelong learning and self-discovery, helping you decide today how you want to live your life moving forward. For some, this may trigger uncomfortable feelings or memories; however, it's important not to use this as a point to feel guilt, frustration, or rumination. Instead, think about what you like about your current situation and what you want to improve in the future. This is called learning. Consider this an opportunity to grow, understand yourself better, and make intentional choices that align with your true values, goals, and desires.

CHAPTER 1
Begin with P.E.A.C.E

I remember the days when I was barely keeping my head above water due to work deadlines, family responsibilities, volunteer obligations, and other commitments that seemed never-ending. The weight of always saying yes led me to being overcommitted, and it felt like I was drowning. The stress was suffocating. I read self-help books, searching for a lifeline, but these books often left me feeling more confused and helpless. I needed real solutions, concrete steps, and practical tips to bring about immediate change.

One evening, after a tough day, I laid back in a chair, gasping for air not from physical exertion, but from the mental exhaustion of trying to honor too many commitments. I had hit my internal brick wall, and I could not do it anymore. In this moment of desperation, I realized something had to change. I needed a structured approach to navigate the chaos and find peace with my decisions. I started small, focusing on learning to pause and evaluate before agreeing to anything.

At first, it felt unnatural to say, "Let me think about it," instead of my usual automatic reply of yes.

With practice, I began to notice a difference. Pausing allowed me to consider whether a new commitment aligned with my values and priorities. Eventually, I found that taking a moment to breathe, reflect, and assess made my decisions more thoughtful and less impulsive. Gradually, I stopped feeling guilty about saying no and started to reclaim my time and energy. Once I confirmed what I would say yes or no to, I was firm and embraced my decision. With a lot of practice, I began to see that I was no longer over-whelmed by a to-do list, and I could focus on things that truly mattered to me.

***

Life is full of twists and turns, and your ability to make wise decisions is essential. This book is a quick and easy resource to help you decide what things will earn your yes and what things will earn your no. The goal is to help you learn what gives you peace, allowing you to make decisions that align with your true values and priorities.

Your lived experiences are unique to you, and while I am going to give you five tips to follow, you will need to do the work of reflecting, journaling, and ultimately deciding the next steps in your life. Throughout this book, you'll find suggestions to guide you.

By now, I hope you're wondering what the five tips are. Brace yourself because they are simple words that can only be amplified by how you choose to apply them in your life. The five words we will explore are pause, evaluate, assess, confirm, and embrace. Each serves a different purpose in the decision -making process, guiding you from the initial reaction to final acceptance with your decision, even if that decision is no.

5 Tips To Unlock Your Life and Find Peace

TIP 1: PAUSE

◊ Take a brief moment to stop and collect your thoughts, preventing impulsive reactions and allowing for mindful reflection.

TIP 2: EVALUATE

◊ Consider the significance and impact of your decision.

◊ Weigh the pros and cons.

◊ Determine if it aligns with your values and goals.

TIP 3: ASSESS

◊ Examine your capabilities, boundaries, and priorities.

◊ Be sure the decision you make supports your goals and aspirations.

TIP 4: CONFIRM

◊ Solidify your choice internally. Is this your final answer or decision?

◊ Reinforce your resolve and commitment to eliminating doubts in the decisions that you made.

TIP 5: EMBRACE

◊ Accept and find peace with your decision.
◊ Let go of any lingering uncertainties and move forward with confidence and contentment.

Each tip builds on the previous one, creating a comprehensive approach to making thoughtful and fulfilling decisions.

Now that you have an overview, let's discuss each tip from a different lens. Specifically,

- What it means
- Why it matters
- When to use it
- What to do
- Where to use it
- How to use it
- Who benefits - this is my favorite - it's YOU!

Tip 1: Pause

What does it mean to pause?

- Pausing allows you to take a brief moment to stop and collect your thoughts before making a decision.

Why is this important?

- Opportunities come in many forms. Many people will ask you to do things. However, you don't always have to say yes. Pausing allows you to avoid impulsive reactions and make thoughtful decisions. You should never allow yourself to feel rushed to give an answer. By taking a moment to pause, you give yourself the chance to process the information you have just received and consider the consequences of your actions. This moment to pause can lead to choices that better reflect your true intentions and values. Impulsive decisions are not always the best decisions, and they often lead to regret or stress; however, a thoughtful approach can help you feel more confident and at peace with your choices. Remember, this is about learning to create a habit of mindfulness in your decision-making process.

When should I pause?

- You should always pause when faced with a decision or request that requires careful consideration. This applies to both major life decisions and everyday choices. Even taking a few seconds for reflection can change the outcome.

- Whenever you feel pressured or unsure, it's a signal that you need to take a step back. Pausing is especially important in situations that trigger emotional responses, as the pause allows you to respond thoughtfully rather than reactively.

What is the pause?

- It's simple. Take a moment to stop, take a deep breath, and collect your thoughts before responding. This simple act of taking a breath can clear your mind and bring focus to your thoughts. It's a small but powerful tool to help you reset and center yourself. In moments of stress or confusion, breathing deeply can reduce anxiety and help you to think more clearly. This practice helps you to approach decisions with a calm and composed mindset.

Where should I pause?

- You can pause anywhere. When possible, find a

quiet safe space or a moment of solitude where you can reflect without distractions. This could be a physical place like a quiet room or a mental space like a brief walk. The environment you choose should allow you to think without interruptions.

- It's important to create a space where you can be alone with your thoughts, even if it's just for a few minutes. This solitude can help you to gain perspective and make more intentional decisions.

How should I pause?

- Simply take a deep breath. Step back mentally, and give yourself the time needed to evaluate the situation. You might find it helpful to close your eyes, count to ten, or practice mindful breathing techniques.

- Give yourself permission to pause, the moment to pause is about creating a buffer between a stimulus and its response, allowing you to approach the situation with clarity. Practicing this regularly can improve your decision-making skills over time. You do not have to rush to respond. Even embracing silence with a long pause can help you.

<u>Who benefits from the pause?</u>

- You benefit by avoiding rushed decisions and responding more thoughtfully. In time and with practice, you will notice that your choices become more aligned with your values and long-term goals. This practice to pause not only benefits you but also those around you, as it can lead to more positive and intentional interactions.

- You don't want to overcommit and underdeliver. Your relationships can improve as others will eventually see you as more considerate and thoughtful when you avoid committing to things that do not serve you well or you cannot follow through on.

- Ultimately, pausing and pondering can enhance your overall quality of life, by fostering a more mindful approach to decision-making.

Tip 2: Evaluate

What does it mean to evaluate?

- To evaluate means to carefully consider all aspects of a decision to understand its significance and impact.

Why should I evaluate?

- Evaluation helps you to understand the significance and impact of your decision. By taking the time to evaluate, you can assess how a choice aligns with your values and long-term goals. This important step prevents you from making decisions based on inadequate information or emotions.

- Evaluating allows you to see the bigger picture and understand the potential outcomes. It's a critical step in ensuring that your decisions contribute positively to your life. Always consider the impact the decision will have on you.

When should I evaluate?

- You must evaluate when presented with a request or decision that requires careful consideration of its implications. This means not rushing into agreements or commitments without fully understanding them. **If you do not understand the request, you should not commit to it.** It's especially important to evaluate decisions that could have long-term effects or require significant time and energy.

- Whenever you feel uncertain or pressured, take a moment after you pause (tip #1) to evaluate (tip #2). This will help you to make more informed and deliberate choices.

What should I evaluate?

- Always analyze requests, weighing the pros, cons and considering whether they align with your personal values. Take time to note both the positive and negative aspects that can result from your decision to say yes versus no. Remember, you must consider how saying yes fits into your life and whether it supports your goals. If it does not fit, consider saying no.

- Analyzing is part of the evaluation process as it also involves thinking about the resources required, such as time, energy, and money. This evaluation should be comprehensive and one that helps you to make a decision that is balanced and well-informed.

Where should I evaluate?

- When possible, engage in evaluation in a calm environment where you can think clearly and objectively. Find a place free from distractions where you can truly focus on the decision at hand. This might be a quiet room, a peaceful outdoor setting, or any place where you feel relaxed and able to think. Find what works for you. The environment plays a significant role in your ability to evaluate effectively. Don't rush this step and make sure that you have the space and time needed to reflect thoroughly.

How should I evaluate?

- Consider the potential outcomes, consequences, and the extent to which the decision supports your goals and values. Think about the short-term and long-term effects of the decision. Ask yourself how this choice aligns with what you truly want and need. Weigh the benefits against the potential drawbacks. This process helps you to see the decision from all angles and ensures that you are making a choice that feels right for you. Taking a systematic approach to evaluation can greatly enhance your decision-making skills.

<u>Who benefits when I evaluate?</u>

- This journey is about you. Never forget you. You benefit by gaining clarity on the importance and implications of decisions that require a yes or a no. This clarity helps you to feel more confident and assured in your choices. It also reduces the likelihood of regret or second-guessing.

- By thoroughly evaluating your options, you ensure that your decisions are intentional and well-considered. This practice not only benefits you but also those around you, as it leads to more positive and thoughtful interactions. Ultimately, evaluation empowers you to make decisions that enhance your overall well-being and align with your values.

TIP 3: ASSESS

What does it mean to assess?

- Assessing means evaluating how a decision aligns with your personal values, priorities, and capabilities.

Why should I assess?

- The assessment step ensures that the decisions you make are aligned with your personal values, priorities, and capabilities. By assessing a decision before you make it, you can determine if the decision you are about to make supports what matters most to you. This step helps you to avoid commitments that might conflict with your principles or even overextend your personal resources. Taking the time to assess can lead to more sustainable and fulfilling choices. This step is about making sure your decisions are in harmony with who you are and what you stand for. Be patient and do not rush this step.

When should I assess?

- It is important to assess after you have evaluated the request and its implications. Once you've taken a moment to pause (tip #1) and evaluate (tip #2) the situation, it's time to take the next step, which is to assess (tip #3) how it fits with your personal framework.

- Always remember that this becomes extremely important when a decision might significantly impact your life or the lives of others. This is your life, and you matter. You must always assess during both major decisions and smaller, everyday choices to ensure consistency. Regular assessment helps you stay true to your values and priorities.

What do I assess?

- Assess your own capabilities, boundaries, finances, resources, and priorities in relation to the decision. Consider whether you have the time, energy, skills, interest, passion, and resources to commit. Think about your boundaries and whether this decision respects them. If the decision does not respect your boundaries, consider using the word "no."
- What I want to reinforce to you is that it's essential to evaluate if your choice aligns with your current priorities, as well as your short-term and long-term goals. Assessing all of these issues helps you to make informed and balanced deci-

sions. This takes practice but ensures you're not over-committing or compromising your own well-being.

Where do I assess?

- Reflect on your values and goals, considering how the decision fits into your larger aspirations. This reflection can take place in a quiet, comfortable environment where you can think deeply. Consider the decision in the context of your overall life plan. Think about how it aligns with your vision for the future and the person you want to become. This perspective is key to making choices that support your long-term aspirations.

How do I assess?

- Reflect on how the decision may impact your life (short-term and long-term) and the lives of others while considering your own needs and limitations. Consider how it might affect your relationships, work, and personal growth. Assess whether the decision supports your needs without overextending yourself. This comprehensive reflection helps you make choices that are both considerate and sustainable. It ensures that your decisions are beneficial for yourself and those around you.

<u>Who benefits when I assess?</u>

- You can always benefit when you assess by en-suring that your decisions are in alignment with your values and priorities. This alignment brings a sense of peace and fulfillment. When your choices reflect your true self, you're more likely to feel satisfied and content. This practice also positively impacts your relationships, as others see you as consistent and reliable. Ultimately, assessing and affirming your decisions enhances your overall well-being and supports a balanced, intentional life.

TIP 4: CONFIRM

What does it mean to confirm?

- Confirming means solidifying your decision internally, providing clarity and confidence in your choice.

Why should I confirm?

- When you finalize your decision you must be firm and confirm. Confirmation reinforces the decision internally, providing clarity and confidence. By confirming your decision, you strengthen your commitment to it and eliminate lingering doubts. This step helps to ensure that you are fully aligned with your choice and prepared to act on it. Reinforcing your decision internally provides a sense of certainty and peace. It helps you to move forward with confidence, knowing that your decision is well-founded.

When do I confirm?

- It's important to confirm after careful evaluation and assessment of the decision. Once you have paused, evaluated, and assessed, it's time to solidify your choice. This is the moment to confirm. This step is the key to ensuring that all aspects of the decision have been thoroughly considered. Confirming after this process ensures that your decision is deliberate and well-considered. Remember to confirm before taking action to avoid second-guessing yourself later.

What do I confirm?

- Confirm your choice and commitment to it, solidifying your resolve. Make a conscious effort to affirm your decision and acknowledge your commitment. This involves embracing your choice wholeheartedly and preparing to follow through. Confirming your decision helps with the transition from contemplation to action. This step is about solidifying your internal agreement with the decision you have made.

Where do I confirm?

- You must confirm within yourself by reaffirming your decision and aligning your thoughts and actions. This process happens internally, as you align your mind and emotions with your choice. It's about creating an internal harmony where your thoughts, feelings, and actions are all in sync. Reflect on your decision and ensure that it resonates with your inner self. This internal alignment is key to maintaining confidence in your choice.

How do I confirm?

- Mentally affirm your decision, reminding your-self of the reasons behind it and the values it re-flects. Take time to reflect on why you made this choice and how it aligns with your values. Reaf-firming these reasons helps to strengthen your resolve and commitment. You might find it help-ful to write down your decision and the reasons behind it. This mental affirmation reinforces your decision and prepares you to act with confidence.

Who benefits when I confirm?

- You can benefit greatly by strengthening your commitment to your decisions. This type of prac-tice enhances your confidence and reduces doubt. By confirming and clarifying your choices, you ensure that they are deliberate and well-founded. This strengthens your ability to follow through and achieve your goals.
- Ultimately, this step leads to greater satisfaction and peace, as you act with more clarity and con-viction in your decisions.

TIP 5: EMBRACE

What does it mean to embrace?

- Embracing means fully accepting your decision and finding peace with it, leading to a sense of closure and contentment.

Why should I embrace?

- Embracing a decision should always bring a sense of closure, acceptance, and peace of mind. By fully accepting your choice, you can move forward without being burdened by doubts or regrets.

- Embracing your decision allows you to feel confident and assured in your actions. This step is crucial for your mental and emotional well-being. Finding peace with your decision helps you to focus on the future rather than dwelling on the past.

When do I embrace?

- It's important to embrace the decision after confirming and moving forward with it. Let your yes or your no be firm and final. Once you pause (tip #1), evaluate (tip #2), assess (tip #3), and confirm your choice (tip #4), it's time to fully accept it and embrace your decision (tip #5).

- This final step ensures that you are ready to take action without hesitation. Embracing your decision is essential before you can truly move forward. It's important to embrace your choice as the final step in the decision-making process.

What do I embrace?

- You must embrace your choice with confidence and acceptance, letting go of doubts or refraining from the temptation to second guess yourself. Fully committing to your decision means letting go of any remaining uncertainties.

- Accept your choice wholeheartedly, knowing that you have made the best possible decision. This involves trusting yourself and your process. Embracing your decision helps you to feel empowered and ready to act.

Where do I embrace?

- You embrace within yourself, finding peace and contentment with your decision. This acceptance happens internally, where you reconcile any internal conflicts. It's about aligning your emotions and thoughts with your choice. Finding peace within yourself is crucial for moving forward confidently. This inner harmony allows you to proceed without internal resistance.

How do I embrace my decision?

- Be sure to make a decision that allows you to let go of any doubts or uncertainties, embracing your choice (regardless of the choice) and moving forward with confidence. Release any negative thoughts or second-guessing that might hold you back.

- Embrace your decision as a positive and intentional choice. This might involve affirmations, mindfulness practices, or simply reminding yourself of the reasons behind your decision. Moving forward with confidence helps you to take decisive and intentional actions.

Who benefits when I embrace?

- You benefit when you embrace by finding peace of mind and contentment with your decisions, leading to greater overall satisfaction and well-being. Embracing your choice reduces stress and anxiety, allowing you to focus on what truly matters. This practice enhances your overall quality of life by fostering a sense of fulfillment and peace. When you are content with your decisions, you can engage more fully and positively in other areas of your life. Ultimately, embracing and exhaling leads to a more balanced and satisfying life.

Conclusion

By understanding and applying these five tips, you have an opportunity to transform your decision-making process into a series of intentional actions. In fact, the more you practice these steps, the more you will learn to be confident in embracing the word "no" when needed. From initial reflection to final acceptance, always ensure that your choices are well-considered and aligned with your values, purpose, and goals. These five tips are a process that is about you and it not only helps you make better decisions but also enhances your overall well-being by providing an opportunity for clarity, confidence, and peace of mind in the decision-making process. As you move forward, remember that the power of saying no is just as important as the power of saying yes. You truly have the power, and this power cannot be taken from you unless you choose to give it away. Giving away your power is also a choice. You must choose wisely. Embrace this five-step process consistently, and you will find yourself more in control and more at ease with the decisions you make.

I wrote this book for you. You are not reading this by chance; it's by choice, and I want you to be equipped with the skills to make conscious, well-thought-out decisions instead of just saying yes for the sake of it. Saying yes to things that don't serve you well has consequences. These consequences can be financial, mental health-related, physical health-related, or can even affect your personal space and well-being. You owe it to yourself to be unapologetic in making yourself and your life a priority. Healthy boundaries are essential, and you cannot say yes all the time. By setting these boundaries and being selective with your commitments, you protect your well-being and ensure that your yes and your no are meaningful and beneficial.

CHAPTER 2
Applying the Five Tips

On the other side of no is an opportunity to be your true authentic self. More important than verbalizing the word no, is knowing when it is appropriate to confidently use it. As introduced in chapter 1, there are five tips to help you determine when to say no: pause, evaluate, assess, confirm, and embrace. Taking the time to first understand this is important. Throughout the remaining chapters we will reinforce the steps in bite size pieces to help equip you with ways to incorporate them into your life. The repetition in this book is intentional. Hearing something one time is not enough. You must practice again and again to familiarize yourself with the steps and eventual application.

No is not negative, sometimes it's necessary. Saying no is far from a negative action; it is a tool for focusing on your personal space and values.

- Have you ever felt guilty when you were told that important projects or endeavors would crumble and fail, if you did not assume the responsibility of group leader?

o   If the answer to this is affirmative, then you (like me and others) have found moments where you overextended yourself.

In a fast-paced and often demanding world, there can be many external demands and expectations. It is the power of choice; deciding where your energy and attention should and should not be focused, makes a difference. Saying no is an affirmation that your mental, emotional, and physical well-being are worth prioritizing. If you find difficulty saying no to others, you might eventually experience depression, burnout, or stress because your overutilization of the word yes results in poor boundaries. The inability to set healthy boundaries can take a toll on your health, happiness, family, work, and overall life.

Moreover, even with this knowledge many hesitate to say no. This can be due to the fear of disappointing others or risking relationships. Despite the rationale, it is essential to understand that self worth is not dependent upon the opinions or expectations of others. You have value, you are a priority, and acknowledging this is the foundation upon which you can build a fulfilling life.

Whether you are a busy professional, a student,

consultant, juggling responsibilities, someone trying to find their path, or at another phase in life, through a series of exercises and techniques, you have an opportunity to use the five tips in this book to help you find the courage to say no and make choices that align with your values and priorities.

Begin by reflecting on instances when you acquiesced to things you did not want to do. I'd like you to consider the following questions to see what you can learn from these experiences.

- How did this make you feel?
- What was the impact on your sense of self and well-being?
- What did you gain or lose by doing this?

The act of reflection is the first step in understanding the value of self-assertion.

Saying no takes practice. Start with small steps. A great place to start practicing saying no is to say no to smaller commitments that do not align with your priorities. Each time you do this, you take a step towards bigger decisions, and you will notice the empowering nature of this simple word.

Clarity and assertiveness are important. You do not need to offer extensive explanations or apologies. A simple "Thank you for thinking of me, but I won't be able to participate" communicates respect and decisiveness. Sometimes an immediate response isn't necessary. Saying "Can I get back to you?" provides space for thoughtful consideration. Think of this as the considered no. Consider the request and decide if it is something that you want to commit to.

The Considered No

1) Evaluate Importance and Alignment

- Life is filled with decisions. Remember, it's impossible to go through the day without making a decision. The ability to evaluate importance and alignment is critical for every decision maker. If the request aligns with your values, goals, and priorities, and it's important for your personal or professional growth, then say yes. If the request conflicts with your values, goals, or priorities, or if it's not essential for your growth or well-being, then say no.

2) Assess Impact and Capacity

- Do you have the capacity to say yes? How will this impact you?
- If accepting the request will have a positive im-

pact on your life or others, and you have the capacity (time, energy, resources) to fulfill it without sacrificing your well-being, then say yes. However, if agreeing to the request will have a negative impact on your life or others, or if you lack the capacity to fulfill it without compromising your well-being, then say no.

3) Consider Boundaries and Limits

- If saying yes maintains healthy boundaries and respects your limits, and it aligns with your personal or professional boundaries, then say yes. If saying yes violates your boundaries, exceeds your limits, or compromises your well-being, then say no.

4) Review Time and Resources

- If you have the time, resources, and energy to commit to the request without neglecting your other responsibilities or priorities, then say yes. If accepting the request would overextend your time or resources, or if it would interfere with your ability to fulfill existing commitments, then say no.

5) Trust Instincts and Gut Feelings

- If your intuition tells you that saying yes feels right and aligns with your inner sense of purpose or fulfillment, then say yes. If your instincts warn you that saying yes doesn't feel right or would lead to discomfort or regret, then say no.

These five tips are the process I like to call the considered no. When you consider the request it allows you time to make a thoughtful and well informed decision. To further illustrate this, below is an algorithm to help you consider how to apply the steps when considering if you should say yes or no. Always pause and reflect before saying yes or no.

Pause and Reflect Before Saying Yes

CONSIDER	YES	NO
Evaluate Importance and Alignment	Does the request align with my values and priorities?	Does the request conflict with my values and priorities?
	(Continue to *Assess* Impact and Capacity)	(Consider saying *no* and stop evaluating further)
Assess Impact and Capacity	Will accepting the request positively impact my life or others'?	Will accepting the request have a negative impact on my life or others'?
	Do I have the capacity to fulfill it without sacrificing my well-being?	Do I lack the capacity to fulfill it without compromising my well-being?
	(Continue to Consider Boundaries and Limits)	(Consider saying *no* and stop evaluating further)
Consider Boundaries and Limits	Does saying *yes* maintain healthy boundaries and respect my limits?	Does saying *yes* violate my boundaries or compromise my well-being?

Consider	Yes	No
	(Continue to Review Time and Resources)	(Consider saying *no* and stop evaluating further)
Review Time and Resources	Do I have the time, resources, and energy to commit without neglecting other responsibilities or priorities?	Would accepting the request overextend my time or resources?
	(Continue to Trust Instincts and Gut Feelings)	(Consider saying *no* and stop evaluating further)
Trust Instincts and Gut Feelings	Does saying *yes* feel right and align with my sense of purpose?	Do my instincts warn me that saying *yes* doesn't feel right?
	(Proceed to Final Decision)	(Proceed to Final Decision)
Final Decision	Say *yes* if all considerations align positively.	Say *no* if any consideration poses significant concerns.

As you build your ability to say no to things that do not serve you well, you may find that you have a more balanced, fulfilled, and empowered life.

Remember, saying no to someone else can be saying yes to essential time needed for your own personal growth, values, and well-being.

CHAPTER 3
The Courage to Say No

The word "no" is beautiful. In the symphony of life, "no" can be the rest note that brings harmony. We often perceive "no" as a harsh word. However, it is important to view it through a different lens. Imagine "no" through the lens that views it as an opportunity that grants space for you to breathe and pause for renewed clarity. "No" is a liberating and affirming word. It's an expression of personal freedom, a safeguard against over-commitment, a guardian of personal boundaries, and an affirmation of self-value. Embracing "no" can be a catalyst for balance for students, professionals, parents, and individuals from all walks of life. Using the word "no" can lead to reduced stress, reduced fatigue, minimized over-commitment, and provide a sense of balance, peace, and control.

Below are some interactive opportunities for you to reflect and journal as you consider ways to optimize your ability to have the courage to say "no."

EXERCISE: REFLECT ON THE EFFECT OF NO

Write about a past instance where you wish you had said no. Write down how saying no might have altered your course of events for the better. This will make it evident how impactful and positive this two-letter word can be.

*If you are in a group, discuss your responses with others.

TECHNIQUE: THE GRACIOUS NO

Saying no does not need to be abrasive. You can learn the art of expressing your no in a courteous way. For instance, you can say, "Thank you for considering me, but unfortunately, I won't be able to take part."

- Practice ways to politely say no. Be gracious.

- Write some examples below and discuss them with others for feedback.

This process takes practice. You can do it!

JOURNAL PROMPT: EMBRACING EMPOWERMENT

Think about a time when saying no made you feel empowered.

- Write down the specifics and the emotions associated with this decision.
    - How did you feel before, during, and after?
    - What does this teach you about the correlation between saying no and your personal power?

JOURNAL PROMPT: PAINTING A PICTURE WITH NO

Visualize your life if you could confidently say no to things that don't align with your values and goals.

- Describe the life you see.
- How does this choice create a sense of balance, fulfillment, and growth?
- Use the space below to write or draw your thoughts.

Once you have the understanding of the beauty of no, you must be able to to assert it. Be assertive: let your no be no.

In every no there is a hidden power. Asserting no is not a simple refusal; it is an affirmation of your identity. It's a clear statement of your values, your boundaries, and your priorities. By asserting no, you don your armor of authenticity, making space for your true self to evolve.

However, it is widely understood that using the word no can be intimidating. The internal questioning, pondering and ruminations can be overwhelming. Sometimes your innate sense of no arises from a desire for self-preservation and dignity. Trust in this inner wisdom because saying no to others can mean saying yes to yourself and your mental well-being. This is something that anyone can relate to, be it a parent, a teenager, an entrepreneur, or anyone who faces daily decisions and social expectations. Developing the ability to assert no is an essential component of productivity, peace of mind, mental, physical and emotional health, and above all self-respect.

As you try asserting no, use these exercises, techniques, and reflective prompts to guide you. Do not simply read them, take time to practice and apply them. You must do the work and commit to learning a new way of thinking.

EXERCISE: ROLE-PLAYING NO

Consider a situation where you usually struggle to say no.

- This could be imaginary or a past scenario.
- Try role-playing, asserting no either by yourself or with a confidant.

This rehearsal will build your stamina for real-life assertiveness.

TECHNIQUE: THE UNYIELDING NO

- When saying no, use a steady tone and maintain assured body language.
- Non-verbal cues are instrumental in reinforcing your verbal message.

JOURNAL PROMPT: STANDING FIRM

Reflect on an instance when you used the word no and held your ground by standing firm in your decision.

- What was the outcome?
- How did it affect your emotions and well-being?
- What did you learn?

Journal Prompt: The Road Not Taken

Think about a moment when you conceded with a yes but wanted to say no.

- What prevented you from saying no?

_____

_____

_____

_____

_____

_____

_____

_____

_____

_____

_____

_____

_____

_____

_____

_____

_____

_____

_____

_____

- With the wisdom of hindsight, how could you have confidently said no?

    - Write some examples below.

_____

_____

_____

_____

_____

_____

_____

_____

_____

_____

_____

_____

_____

_____

_____

_____

_____

_____

_____

_____

Asserting the word no is more than just a response, it's self-empowerment and takes courage. It's an exercise in trusting your own voice. Your no is liberating. Once you assert the word no, there are times when a natural positive response evolves. Every no directed at negativity is a yes to your wellness, renewal, and inner peace.

Saying no can be good for your soul. It facilitates emotional, mental, and physical revival.

- Does saying yes deplete you, cause your increased stress, or devalue you?
  - **Say no.**

Yet, for many of us, the prospect of setting boundaries and prioritizing oneself can be a new concept. Your initial decision to choose this self-empowerment might be accompanied by feelings of guilt or discomfort. However, know that this discomfort stems from the unfamiliarity of putting yourself first. With perseverance, you will see this discomfort give way to liberation and an act of self-love. Societal pressures often dictate a need for acceptance and validation, which can lead to saying yes more than we should. Healing begins once you understand that love and respect start within.

Take an opportunity to practice the exercises below to guide you:

EXERCISE: MIRROR AFFIRMATIONS

- Stand in front of a mirror and focus your eyes on your reflection. Speak the word no assertively.
- Practice this daily. This is not a practice of denial but rather an exercise in familiarity with the strength and empowerment carried in the word.
- Believe in your ability to say no.

TECHNIQUE: THE CONSIDERED NO

- When presented with requests or demands that cause you discomfort, take a step back. Reflect on its impact on your well-being.
- If it does not foster positivity, firmly say no.

JOURNAL PROMPT: SHIFTING PERSPECTIVES

- Think of an occasion where you neglected your needs for someone else's.
- Document your emotions and thoughts from that time.

- Then, reimagine the scenario with you choosing no.
- How does this alter your emotions?

_____

_____

_____

_____

_____

_____

_____

_____

_____

_____

_____

_____

_____

_____

_____

_____

_____

_____

_____

- Think of an occasion where you neglected your needs for someone else's.
- Document your emotions and thoughts from that time. Then, reimagine the scenario with you choosing no.
- How does this alter your emotions?

_____

_____

_____

_____

_____

_____

_____

_____

_____

_____

_____

_____

_____

_____

_____

_____

_____

_____

JOURNAL PROMPT: FACING FEARS

What would life be like if you confront your fears associated with saying no?

- Whether it be anxiety of rejection, judgment, or loss of affection, write about these fears below and identify ways you can bring them to light and confront them.

Recognition is the first stop on the path to healing. Beginning on a path to utilize the power of no can be transformative. Take time to remind yourself that your safety, worth, and well-being are important. You are complete, with or without your agreement to, or compliance with, things that you would rather not do. The key to your renewal rests in the strength of your ability to effectively utilize the word no.

CHAPTER 4

There is Power in Your No

The Garden of Life

When my youngest son and I set out to start our home garden, we were excited. On the first day, we planted our seedlings, wondering if the garden would grow. My son mentioned that the plants weren't spaced well, but I trusted my limited knowledge and proceeded as planned. Later, a friend who visited confirmed my son's observation, pointing out that we hadn't spaced them correctly and they wouldn't thrive as they were. My son smiled knowingly, and I realized he had been right all along.

Determined to get it right, we went back to the store, bought more soil, and replanted the seedlings, ensuring each seedling had enough room to grow. As we worked, I remembered the gardening lessons my mother had passed on to my four children before she passed away. My son, holding to these teachings, insisted on following the methods he had learned from her. In the midst of our adjustments, I called a friend from Trinidad for advice. Over the phone, she shared her wisdom, encouraging us to find what truly worked for our garden. Despite all the external advice, the final decision to replant and rearrange the garden was ours.

After replanting, my son decided to take it a step further by building a greenhouse. This was not just a physical structure, but a safe place where the plants would be protected and nurtured. Day by day, he tended to the garden, discovering what worked best for each seedling, now turned into plants. When certain methods didn't achieve the desired results, he didn't hesitate to change his approach. His dedication ensured that the plants grew and thrived, rather than merely surviving.

We began collecting rainwater for the plants, carefully monitored their growth, and adjusted their care as needed. Every day, I would video-conference with my friend from Trinidad and her son. They were amazed at the progress of our garden and asked what we were doing to achieve such success. I shared the lessons we had learned and the power of consistency. It became clear that, just like in life, we had to find our own path, what worked best for our plants.

Even my husband's friend doubted us, saying it was too late in the season to start a garden and that nothing would grow. But we stood firm. Not only did our plants grow, they provided us with fresh greens, herbs, and lettuces that reduced our need to go to the grocery store. Watching my son enjoy the salads we made from our garden was amazing. We nurtured the garden, and it nurtured us back, bringing us closer as a family and filling our home with fresh, healthy food.

This experience taught me ten valuable lessons about the power of "no" and nurturing our own lives:

1. **Space to Grow:** Just like plants need space to grow, we need to set boundaries to thrive.
2. **Trust Your Instincts:** My son trusted what he had learned from his grandmother, and it paid off. Trust your inner wisdom.
3. **Adapt and Change:** When something doesn't work, don't be afraid to change your approach.
4. **Find Your Path:** While advice is valuable, ultimately, you need to find what works for you.
5. **Consistency is Key:** Regular care and attention yield the best results.
6. **Nurture Daily:** Just like a garden needs daily care, so does your well-being.
7. **Learn and Share:** Sharing what you learn can help others.
8. **Embrace New Methods:** Don't be afraid to try new things and innovate.
9. **Celebrate Growth:** Recognize and celebrate your progress and growth even if it is like a gar-

den and takes time.

10. **No Looking Back:** Focus on what works and keep moving forward without dwelling on past failures.

From this journey, I also realized the importance of finding peace in our decisions. My garden gives me peace. As introduced in Chapter 1, here's how the P.E.A.C.E acronym can be applied to both gardening and life:

TIP 1: PAUSE

- Take a brief moment to stop and collect your thoughts, preventing impulsive reactions and allowing for mindful reflection, just like giving your garden a moment to settle and grow.

- Be patient: We had to pause and consider what we were going to do. Everyone has advice, but it's not always the advice for us. What would have happened if everyone had a negative comment and we listened? You cannot prevent people from being negative but you have the power to choose what you will or will not do with the information they share.

TIP 2: EVALUATE

- Consider the significance and impact of your decision. Weigh the pros and cons.

- Determine if it aligns with your values and goals; much like evaluating the needs of each plant in your garden.

- Are you taking the time to evaluate what's best for your growth?

TIP 3: ASSESS

- Examine your capabilities, boundaries, and priorities.

- Be sure the decision you make supports your goals and aspirations; similar to assessing the growth requirements of your garden.

- Are you assessing your needs and capabilities to support your goals?

TIP 4: CONFIRM

- Solidify your choice internally. Is this your final

answer or decision?

- Reinforce your resolve and commitment to eliminating doubts in the decisions that you made; just as you would confirm the best care methods for your garden. We confirmed what worked.
- What would have happened if we kept changing based on what others said we should do?

TIP 5: EMBRACE

- Accept and find peace with your decision.

- Let go of any lingering uncertainties and move forward with confidence and contentment; like embracing the growth and changes in your garden.

- When we found peace with our decision, we stayed focused.

- Are you embracing and finding peace with your decisions?

Remember, each of the five tips builds on the previous one, creating an approach to making thoughtful and fulfilling decisions. Just like in our garden, finding what worked for us and nurturing it consistently led to thriving and growth. Using your no can help you thrive, not just survive.

In every no, there is a hidden yes to self-growth, which cultivates the seeds of self-love and courage. Think of your life as a garden. The seeds you sow and nurture today determine the blooms in your garden tomorrow. One of the most nurturing seeds you can sow is the seed of no. With each no to elements that do not enrich you, you affirm a yes to your evolution. In doing so, you nurture the seeds of self-love and bravery, allowing them to blossom. It is imperative to acknowledge that just like any living entity be it a garden, an animal, or a forest we often crave and deserve nurturing. The time and effort invested in nurturing ourselves should match, if not surpass, the care we extend to our belongings. Ultimately, your well-being must be a priority; you are entitled to thrive and grow.

To facilitate your journey in **nurturing** your life with the power of no the exercises, techniques, and journal prompts below are recommended for your review. Take time to reflect as you go through each exercise. This time is about you.

EXERCISE: CULTIVATING THE NURTURING NO

- Identify a habit or routine that depletes your energy or stops your growth.
  - Commit to say no to it and replace it with an activity that nourishes you.

_____

_____

_____

_____

TECHNIQUE: THE NURTURING PAUSE

- Before agreeing to any request or demand, pause and reflect.
  - Ask yourself, does this align with your well-being or does it drain you?
  - Allow this moment of introspection to guide the response you choose.

_____

_____

_____

_____

JOURNAL PROMPT: DOCUMENTING GROWTH

- Take a moment to reflect upon an instance when saying no helped with personal growth.
  - How did it reshape you?
  - What emotions and insights did it bring to light?

_____

_____

_____

_____

JOURNAL PROMPT: TAKE CARE OF YOUR GARDEN

- Visualize your life as a garden. Identify the weeds (negative influences or draining commitments) that need uprooting through no.
  - Describe how this will cultivate a more fertile and enriching garden.

_____

_____

_____

_____

The art of saying no is an essential component of mental health and self-care. Nurture yourself by embracing the word "no." Nurturing is like an art. It is not about indiscriminately saying yes; rather, it is about selective nurturing—making conscious choices that foster your growth. Realize that the effort you extend to your possessions and external commitments is equally, if not more, deserved by your own well-being. The empowering no you speak today will nurture the flourishing garden of your tomorrow.

Courage is often associated with heroic acts in the face of danger. However, courage can also be found in the subtleties of everyday life, such as asserting a no when your peace or values are at stake. Saying no does not equate to failure; it signifies that priorities might shift and alternative routes might be taken. You have the right to change your mind. The world adapts, and life moves forward. When no is the guardian of your peace and well-being, it is not simply an option—it becomes an imperative; in fact, it can be a solution.

EXERCISE: THE NO EXPEDITION

- Begin by challenging yourself to say no at least

once daily for a week.

- Whether it's declining an additional task at work or taking a stand against something contrary to your values, carefully observe and witness the empowerment this brings.

TECHNIQUE: TAKE A BREATHER

- If you are uncertain whether to say no, request a moment to contemplate; this is a breather.
  - A breather equips you with the pause and space needed to find your courage and to go for what truly serves you.

JOURNAL PROMPT: HAVE COURAGE

- Reflect on an experience where your no was a testament to courage. Describe the emotions it elicited and its repercussions on both you and the surrounding circumstances.
- For every action there is a reaction.
  - What was the outcome?

_____

_____

_____

_____

JOURNAL PROMPT: RECLAIMING YOUR POWER

- Think about a moment where you reluctantly agreed with a yes but actually yearned for the bravery to say no.
  - What prevented you from declining?
  - How can you reclaim your power and say no in future challenging situations?

_____

_____

_____

_____

Using the word no when facing unreasonable requests at work, community, and other places leads to increased mental well-being. Have the courage to be balanced. Place trust in your decisions, let your no be firm. Do not question yourself once you make a decision. You may observe that your life moves towards balance and fulfillment.

CHAPTER 5

Embracing the Power of No
THE POWER OF NO IN ACTION

A few years ago, I was serving as the vice president of a local organization. I had committed over 20 hours a month to the role over a two-year period. When the two-year term ended, I was asked to run for president. Many members believed I was the perfect fit to lead the organization to new heights. Initially, I felt flattered and seriously considered it.

However, as I thought about the commitment, I realized the presidency would require even more time and energy than the vice presidency. Meetings often took place at night and on weekends, encroaching on family time. I would be on late calls, even during my son's swim meets, and the role demanded constant attention to reports and administrative tasks. It left little room for my personal goals and dreams, such as youth leadership development, teaching cardiopulmonary resuscitation (CPR), writing books, and engaging in speaking opportunities.

Despite the recognition and the potential impact of the role, I had to weigh it against my well-being and aspirations. I paused to reflect on the situation. Was this position in alignment with my values and goals, or would it sacrifice my personal dreams for the sake of the organization? I evaluated the significance and impact of my decision, considering how it would affect my time with family and my personal growth. I assessed my capabilities and priorities, recognizing that my true passion lay in youth leadership, writing, and speaking, not in the demanding administrative tasks of the presidency.

After much reflection, I confirmed my decision not to run for president. Instead, I chose to focus on what mattered to me. When I communicated my decision, I was met with surprise and some disappointment. One person even told me it was career suicide not to run for office. But I didn't let that influence me one bit. I was firm in my decision and felt a profound sense of peace. This choice allowed me to invest in my personal goals and spend quality time with my family, ultimately leading to a more fulfilling and balanced life. I could have run for vice president again or even president, but it wasn't in alignment with my true goals and aspirations.

Interestingly, around the same time, my son was also nominated for the vice president position of the teen group within the same organization. He had seen firsthand the toll my responsibilities had taken on our family time. When he was asked to run, he surprised me by declining the nomination. I actually encouraged him to reconsider, but he didn't hesitate or look back. His decision was firm, and he later told me that he was happy I wasn't going to run for an office either, as it would have conflicted with his swim meets. His enthusiasm for swimming and our time together mattered most to him.

This experience reinforced a profound lesson for me: our families spell love as time. They want and need our presence more than anything else. We can show love by making time for them; they must be the priority. By saying no to commitments that detract from our time with them, we prioritize what truly matters. My son's excitement about our decision showed me that the quality moments we spend with our loved ones far outweigh any prestigious title or role. It was a reminder that sometimes, the most powerful word we can use is no, to protect our time and our well-being.

From this journey, I learned ten valuable lessons about the power of no:

1. **Family First**: Prioritizing family time over additional commitments ensures stronger relationships and cherished memories.
2. **Health Matters**: Your mental, emotional, and

physical well-being should always take precedence.

3. **True Passion**: Focus on what you are truly passionate about and what brings you joy.

4. **Evaluate Priorities**: Assess the impact of new commitments on your existing responsibilities and goals.

5. **Quality Over Quantity**: It's better to excel in fewer roles than to be overwhelmed by many.

6. **Boundaries are Essential**: Setting boundaries helps maintain balance and prevents burnout.

7. **Courage to Say No**: It takes courage to decline roles, even prestigious ones, to protect your well-being.

8. **Lead by Example**: Demonstrating the importance of saying no can inspire others, including your children.

9. **Long-term Vision**: Consider how your decisions today affect your long-term goals and aspirations.

10. **Self-Worth**: Recognize that you are worthy of prioritizing your needs and desires.

I used the five tips for P.E.A.C.E to make my decision:

TIP 1: PAUSE

- Take a brief moment to stop and collect your thoughts, preventing impulsive reactions and allowing for mindful reflection.
  - This pause was crucial for me to understand the impact the presidency would have on my life.
  - Reflecting back on that moment of stillness, I asked myself, "What would happen if I didn't take this time to reflect?"
  - This pause gave me the clarity to see the bigger picture and prioritize my well-being.

TIP 2: EVALUATE

- Consider the significance and impact of your decision. Weigh the pros and cons, determining if the role aligns with your values and goals.
  - I had asked myself, "Am I taking the time to evaluate what's best for my growth?" and "Do I really want to do this, or am I doing this because people want and expect me to?"
  - This evaluation helped me realize that while the presidency was prestigious for some, it did not align with my personal aspirations

and would compromise my family time and personal passions.

TIP 3: ASSESS

- Examine your capabilities, boundaries, and priorities.
  - I had to assess if taking on the presidency would support my goals and aspirations or detract from them.
  - I reflected deeply on my needs and whether this demanding role would help or hinder my growth.
  - This honest assessment reinforced the importance of staying true to my personal goals and boundaries.

TIP 4: CONFIRM

- Solidify your choice internally. Ask yourself if this is your final decision and reinforce your resolve to eliminate doubts.
  - I asked myself, "Is this truly my final answer?"
  - Reflecting on the potential consequences of changing my decision based on others' opin-

ions and expectations helped me stand firm.

- This internal confirmation brought me a sense of conviction and peace.

TIP 5: EMBRACE

- Accept and find peace with your decision. Letting go of lingering uncertainties allows you to move forward with confidence and contentment.
  - Embracing my decision to prioritize my family and personal well-being over external validation brought me immense peace. I asked myself, "Am I embracing and finding peace with my decision?"
  - This embrace of my choice allowed me to move forward with a clear and confident heart.

While learning about the power of saying no, you have explored the many ways that this word liberates, heals, and nurtures. The humble no, only two letters, has an impact. Through embracing no, we enter the realm where our well-being takes precedence over external pressures and demands. This is a great place to be.

Saying no is not an indication of unwillingness

to cooperate; rather, it's a necessary act of self-preservation when cooperation comes at the cost of your well-being and what serves you best. Prioritizing your needs is not an act of selfishness; rather, it is a step in maintaining your mental, emotional, and physical health. Some people may accuse you of being selfish when you assert your boundaries, but it's essential to use the P.E.A.C.E. method to evaluate these situations. Pause to reflect on the request. Evaluate if it serves someone else well but sacrifices you. Assess if the decision aligns with your values and capacity. Confirm your decision based on your priorities. Embrace your choice with confidence. By setting boundaries and understanding your limits, you ensure that your contributions remain sustainable and meaningful. Making yourself a priority is essential for long-term success and happiness, and it allows you to be the best version of yourself for those around you.

As you go forward, integrating the five tips of the P.E.A.C.E. acronym, keep in mind that with practice and perseverance you will get stronger at declining things that you do not want to do. The art of rejecting what does not serve you well actually equips you with the fortitude to affirm what actually nourishes your soul. You must take time for yourself, enjoy life, and spend time in places that make you feel happy, peaceful, and joyous. Be careful with what you say yes to, and when needed, do not be afraid to say no. You deserve it. You are worthy. Think about spreading the power of no. If you know others who might find comfort or strength in these words, guide them to read this book and encourage them to use the five tips for P.E.A.C.E. that you are taking by applying the concepts in this book. Appreciate and use the strength hidden within this short word, made up of just two letters: N and O. The power to say no resides within you. It serves as your compass (guiding you), your armor (protecting you), and your key (unlocking your true potential). Use your no—your compass, armor, and key—wisely and purposefully. With this in mind, may your no's be frequent, your regrets few, and may you keep your spirit focused with energy to complete the assignment that you were called to do.

CHAPTER 6

Take Charge of Your Life with the Ultimate Power Move

OVERCOMING THE FEAR OF MISSING OUT

When I first started learning to say no, it felt like a huge challenge. Every time I was presented with an opportunity or request, a part of me feared missing out on something important or exciting. This fear often led me to say yes, even when it wasn't in my best interest. Each time I agreed to something I knew I should decline, I became angry with myself. Frustration and self-doubt filled my mind. Why couldn't I just stop saying yes?

In one particular instance, I had been passionate about serving on the board of directors for a local organization I cared deeply about. Excitedly, I turned in my nomination profile for a board of directors position, anticipating the opportunity to make an impact. However, when the slate of nominees was announced, I was listed as the candidate for treasurer instead. I felt a mix of anger, frustration, and confusion. Why had my aspirations been overlooked? I was clear in what I wanted to do and I was qualified, but they needed a treasurer, so they put their needs above my desires. I made it clear that I did not want to do this, but they did not listen.

Despite knowing I should say no, I felt an overwhelming need to say yes. I knew I didn't need another position in any organization but convinced myself that this role was better than no role at all to be close to my goal of being a director on the board. So, I went through with it and was elected as treasurer. However, with every meeting, it became increasingly clear that this was not where I wanted to serve. The responsibilities were draining, and I felt minimal passion for the tasks at hand. I also felt like a hypocrite, contradicting the advice I often gave to others about finding balance and prioritizing their well-being.

Shortly after assuming the role, I began to dread each meeting and interaction related to this position. I realized that continuing to sacrifice my time and energy in a position that didn't align with my goals was the worst thing I could do. I felt trapped and unhappy, but the fear of letting others down kept me from speaking up.

One night, after yet another exhausting meeting, I made a decision. I chose to prioritize my well-being over the perceived obligation. I decided to resign. The moment I made this choice, I felt an overwhelming sense of relief. As I typed my resignation letter, my heart lightened. When I finally hit send on the email, I felt so much happiness and freedom come over me. I knew I had made the right decision.

Resigning from the treasurer position taught me a lesson. Sacrificing myself for a role that didn't fulfill me was not worth the toll it took on my health and happiness. Choosing to step down allowed me to regain control of my time and focus on what truly mattered to me. It reminded me that it's never too late to take control of your life and find your peace.

This experience showed me the power of saying no. It's not just about declining an offer; it's about affirming what is important in your life. By saying no to the treasurer position, I said yes to my well-being. I learned that sometimes, the most powerful and liberating choice we can make is to say no to what doesn't serve us, and in doing so, we create space for what does.

Through this journey, I also discovered that the initial struggle and discomfort of saying no are worth the peace and fulfillment. This story isn't only about learning to say no; it's about finding the courage to choose what's best for you, even when it's hard. It's about realizing that you deserve to live a life that aligns with your true self and that it's never too late to make that choice. Stay in control, and always seek your peace. Remember, the art of saying no requires practice. Give yourself grace and try again. You will get stronger with each attempt. Keep practicing until you learn to confidently and consistently use the word no when you need to.

Here are ten lessons about the power of no from this experience:

1. **Clarity in Communication**: Always be clear about your aspirations and boundaries from the beginning to avoid misunderstandings.
2. **Self-Validation:** Trust your own judgment and don't let others' needs overshadow your desires.
3. **Emotional Awareness:** Recognize feelings of anger and frustration as signals that something isn't aligned with your values.
4. **Importance of Passion:** Participate in roles and activities that you are passionate about to maintain motivation and fulfillment.
5. **Energy Management:** Pay attention to how your commitments affect your energy levels and overall well-being.
6. **Consistent Reflection:** Regularly assess your commitments to ensure they align with your goals and values. If they don't have the courage to change.

7. **Courage to Speak Up:** Don't be afraid to voice your discomfort or dissatisfaction with a role or commitment.

8. **Freedom in Letting Go:** Understand that resigning from a misaligned role can bring immense relief and happiness.

9. **Health Over Obligation:** Prioritize your health and well-being over perceived obligations to others.

10. **Continuous Practice:** Mastering the art of saying no takes practice, self-compassion, and perseverance.

To elaborate further, I used the P.E.A.C.E. method to make my decision:

TIP 1: PAUSE

- Take a brief moment to stop and collect your thoughts, preventing impulsive reactions and allowing for mindful reflection.
    - When I was first asked to take the treasurer position, I failed to pause and truly reflect on whether this role aligned with my aspirations and well-being.
    - Later, I realized the importance of pausing

and recognized that it did not align with my goals.

- It was not too late to pause and make a change, so I decided to step back and reconsider my commitments.

TIP 2: EVALUATE

- Consider the significance and impact of your decision. Weigh the pros and cons, determining if the role aligns with your values and goals.
  - Initially, I didn't thoroughly evaluate the treasurer position.
  - When I finally took the time to evaluate, I asked myself, "Am I taking the time to evaluate what's best for my growth?" and "Do I really want to do this, or am I doing this because people want and expect me to?" This evaluation helped me realize that the position did not align with my true aspirations.
  - It was not too late to evaluate my decision and choose a path that better suited my goals.

TIP 3: ASSESS

- Examine your capabilities, boundaries, and priorities.
  - Initially, I didn't assess my capabilities and boundaries effectively.
  - Later, I realized that continuing to sacrifice my time and energy in a position that didn't align with my goals was the worst thing I could do.
  - It was not too late to assess my situation and decide to resign, which ultimately supported my well-being and personal growth.

TIP 4: CONFIRM

- Solidify your choice internally. Ask yourself if this is your final decision and reinforce your resolve to eliminate doubts.
  - Initially, I did not confirm my choice with confidence.
  - When I finally did, I asked myself, "Is this truly my final answer?" Reflecting on the potential consequences of changing my decision based on others' opinions and expectations helped me stand firm in my choice to resign.

- It was not too late to confirm my decision and move forward with certainty.

Tip 5: Embrace

Accept and find peace with your decision. Letting go of lingering uncertainties allows you to move forward with confidence and contentment. Initially, I struggled to embrace my decision. When I finally did, embracing my decision to resign and prioritize my well-being brought me immense peace and a sense of freedom. It was not too late to embrace my choice and find the peace I needed.

Remember, the journey to mastering the art of saying no requires practice. Give yourself grace and try again. Each attempt brings you closer to a life that truly reflects your values and aspirations. Keep practicing until you learn to confidently and consistently use no when you need to.

Bonus Workbook:
30-Day Action Plan for
No Is A Complete Sentence:
5 Tips To Unlock Your Life and Find Peace

Welcome to a 30-Day Action Plan, designed to complement your reading of *Embrace Your No: 5 Tips to Unlock Your Life and Find Peace.* This plan is designed to empower you to take specific action over the next 30 days. Reflect on your current situation and identify areas where you want to grow and make positive changes.

- Use the space below to journal and reflect. As you read this book, you discovered the power within you to choose when to say yes or no in order to create a life aligned with your values.
- Go back and revisit the chapters of this book, this is not a one time read, you should read this book more than once and use the 30-day action below multiple times.
- You can use this action plan independently or with a group of friends or colleagues who have also read this book. Having accountability partners as you apply these five tips to unlock your life and find peace can be helpful.

Throughout this action plan, you will receive practical guidance and actionable steps for each day. By implementing these strategies, the goal is for you to gradually gain confidence and experience the transformative impact of saying no with intention. Never forget that each day presents an opportunity for personal growth and empowerment. Take charge of your life and release the true potential that lies within you.

DAY 1: INTENTION SETTING

- Set a clear intention for this 30-day journey.
  - Write down what you hope to achieve by incorporating the power of no into your life.

_____

_____

_____

_____

_____

_____

_____

_____

_____

_____

_____

_____

_____

_____

_____

_____

_____

_____

_____

_____

_____

DAY 2: REFLECT ON YOUR CURRENT YES

- Reflect on your current commitments and responsibilities.
    - Make a list of what you usually say yes to,
    even if you'd rather not.

_____

_____

_____

_____

_____

_____

_____

_____

_____

_____

_____

_____

_____

_____

_____

_____

_____

_____

_____

DAY 3: IDENTIFY YOUR VALUES

- Identify your core values.
    - Include what matters most to you. This will help you in deciding when to say no.

_____

_____

_____

_____

_____

_____

_____

_____

_____

_____

_____

_____

_____

_____

_____

_____

_____

_____

DAY 4: READ CHAPTER 1

- Review Chapter 1. Reflect on how it resonates with your experiences.

  - Identify what you learned and how you plan to implement at least three things from the chapter.

_____

_____

_____

_____

_____

_____

_____

_____

_____

_____

_____

_____

_____

_____

_____

_____

_____

DAY 5: PRACTICE SAYING NO

- Practice saying no to something small that does-n't align with your values or interests.

_____

_____

_____

_____

_____

_____

_____

_____

_____

_____

_____

_____

_____

_____

_____

_____

_____

_____

_____

DAY 6: JOURNALING

- Write about your experience of saying no so far.
  - How did it make you feel?
  - What are the positive results that came from this experience that you want to replicate in the future?

_____

_____

_____

_____

_____

_____

_____

_____

_____

_____

_____

_____

_____

_____

_____

_____

_____

_____

_____

DAY 7: SEEK SUPPORT

- Share your goal of having more confidence to say no with a friend or family member who can be your support system throughout this journey.
  - Be clear and concise when sharing your goal of practicing the ability to decline things.
  - Write what you specifically want them to help you with as an accountability partner.

_____

_____

_____

_____

_____

_____

_____

_____

_____

_____

_____

_____

_____

_____

_____

_____

DAY 8: READ CHAPTER 2

- Review Chapter 2
- Write three things that you learned about the importance of saying no.

_____

_____

_____

_____

_____

_____

_____

_____

_____

_____

_____

_____

_____

_____

_____

_____

_____

_____

_____

_____

_____

DAY 9: SELF-REFLECTION

- Reflect on instances in the past where saying no could have benefited you.
  - Write them below.

_____

_____

_____

_____

_____

_____

_____

_____

_____

_____

_____

_____

_____

_____

_____

_____

_____

_____

_____

_____

DAY 10: SET BOUNDARIES

- Start setting small boundaries in personal relationships or at work.

  - Write down the specific things that you will focus on today.

_____

_____

_____

_____

_____

_____

_____

_____

_____

_____

_____

_____

_____

_____

_____

_____

_____

_____

_____

Day 11: Reinforce Your No

- Practice reinforcing your no if someone tries to persuade you otherwise.
  - Write about this experience and what you learned about the importance of reinforcing non-participation in things that you do not want to do.

_____

_____

_____

_____

_____

_____

_____

_____

_____

_____

_____

_____

_____

_____

_____

_____

_____

DAY 12: REWARD YOURSELF

- Write a list of ways that you can celebrate your progress.

  - Do at least one thing for yourself as a reward for setting boundaries and making progress toward your goal of saying no.

_____

_____

_____

_____

_____

_____

_____

_____

_____

_____

_____

_____

_____

_____

_____

_____

_____

DAY 13: READ CHAPTER 3

- Review Chapter 3 of the book.
  - Write what you learned that you can apply to your life.
  - What are your specific thoughts?

_____

_____

_____

_____

_____

_____

_____

_____

_____

_____

_____

_____

_____

_____

_____

_____

_____

_____

_____

Day 14: Practice Self-Care

- Say no to something draining and use that time for self-care instead.

  - Write a list of things that you want to do for your self-care and try one self-care activity today.

_____

_____

_____

_____

_____

_____

_____

_____

_____

_____

_____

_____

_____

_____

_____

_____

_____

DAY 15: CONNECT WITH OTHERS

- Identify a group or forum where others are also working on setting boundaries and saying no.

_____

_____

_____

_____

_____

_____

_____

_____

_____

_____

_____

_____

_____

_____

_____

_____

_____

_____

_____

DAY 16: READ CHAPTER 4

- Review Chapter 4 of the book.
  - What did you learn?

_____

_____

_____

_____

_____

_____

_____

_____

_____

_____

_____

_____

_____

_____

_____

_____

_____

DAY 17: NURTURING ACTION

- Take one action that nurtures your personal growth.
    - Write about what you learned.

_____

_____

_____

_____

_____

_____

_____

_____

_____

_____

_____

_____

_____

_____

_____

_____

_____

_____

_____

DAY 18: EVALUATE YOUR PROGRESS

- Evaluate the progress you've made so far.
  - How has saying no impacted your life?
  - Write specific examples that you are most proud of.

_____

_____

_____

_____

_____

_____

_____

_____

_____

_____

_____

_____

_____

_____

_____

_____

_____

_____

DAY 19: READ CHAPTER 5

- Review Chapter 5 of the book and reflect on the courage in saying no.
  - Write down at least 3 courageous actions that you will take in the next twenty-four hours.

_____

_____

_____

_____

_____

_____

_____

_____

_____

_____

_____

_____

_____

_____

_____

_____

_____

_____

DAY 20: BRAVE NO

- Take a courageous step by saying no to something significant that doesn't serve you.
  - Write about the importance of bravery.

_____
_____
_____
_____
_____
_____
_____
_____
_____
_____
_____
_____
_____
_____
_____
_____
_____
_____
_____
_____

DAY 21: SHARE YOUR STORY

- Share your experience with someone close to you.
  - How has this journey changed you so far?

_____

_____

_____

_____

_____

_____

_____

_____

_____

_____

_____

_____

_____

_____

_____

_____

_____

_____

_____

_____

DAY 22: EMBRACE THE POSITIVE

- Embrace the positive changes in your life that have resulted from saying no.

_____

_____

_____

_____

_____

_____

_____

_____

_____

_____

_____

_____

_____

_____

_____

_____

_____

_____

_____

_____

DAY 23: READ THE CONCLUSION

- Read the last chapter of this book for final insights and motivation.

  - Write about what you learned that you will apply to your life.

_____

_____

_____

_____

_____

_____

_____

_____

_____

_____

_____

_____

_____

_____

_____

_____

_____

DAY 24: CREATE YOUR MANTRA

- Create a personal mantra that empowers you to say no when needed.
  - Examples of mantras:
    - "I respect my time and energy."

    - "I will say no when needed."

    - "I am confident in my choices."

    - "I will say no to allow me to protect my peace and focus on my well-being."

    - "My time is valuable."

    - "I have the strength to say no to anything that doesn't serve my goals and priorities."

_____

_____

_____

_____

_____

_____

_____

_____

_____

DAY 25: PAY IT FORWARD

- Encourage someone else who might benefit from learning to say no.
  - Write down the names of people you plan to encourage.

_____

_____

_____

_____

_____

_____

_____

_____

_____

_____

_____

_____

_____

_____

_____

_____

_____

_____

_____

DAY 26: REFLECT ON YOUR YES

- Reflect and write about the things you can now say yes to because you've learned to say no.

_____

_____

_____

_____

_____

_____

_____

_____

_____

_____

_____

_____

_____

_____

_____

_____

_____

_____

_____

_____

Day 27: Commit to Continual Growth

- Make a commitment to continually reassess and establish boundaries as your life evolves.
  - Write a list of commitments to yourself.

Examples:

1. Commitment to Self-Care
- I commit to prioritizing my mental and physical health by planning 30 minutes each day for self-care activities, specifically meditation, exercise, and relaxation.

2. Commitment to Personal Growth
- I commit to personal development by scheduling 2 hours each week to reading a book related to my personal growth.

3. Commitment to Relationships
- I commit to nurturing healthy relationships with my family by having a dedicated phone-free family dinner at least three times a week prior to 6:00pm.

4. Commitment to Work-Life Balance
- I commit to maintaining a healthy work-life balance by not working beyond 6:00pm on weekdays and not working on the weekends.

5. Commitment to Saying No
- I commit to saying no to at least one request

or obligation each week that does not align with my values or priorities.

_____

_____

_____

_____

_____

_____

_____

_____

_____

_____

_____

_____

_____

_____

_____

_____

_____

_____

_____

_____

DAY 28: CELEBRATE

- Write a list of your achievements over the past 28 days.

  - Celebrate your achievements over the past month with a small get-together or treat.

_____

_____

_____

_____

_____

_____

_____

_____

_____

_____

_____

_____

_____

_____

_____

_____

_____

_____

DAY 29: PLAN AHEAD

- Write a list of how you will continue to incorporate the power of no in the months ahead.

_____

_____

_____

_____

_____

_____

_____

_____

_____

_____

_____

_____

_____

_____

_____

_____

_____

_____

_____

_____

_____

DAY 30: GRATITUDE AND REFLECTION

- Write a letter to yourself expressing gratitude for the work you've put into this 30-day journey.

    - Reflect on how you've grown and how you will continue to use the power of no to unlock your yes.

_____

_____

_____

_____

_____

_____

_____

_____

_____

_____

_____

_____

_____

_____

_____

_____

_____

CHAPTER 7
Unlock Your Life: You Are A Priority

Cultivating a habit where "yes" is the common theme did not happen overnight; this was a learned behavior. You are now unlearning the overutilization of your "yes" to please others and relearning life when you use the power of your "no" to please you. As you continue taking charge of your life by embracing the power of no, you must equip yourself with the necessary tools for success. The list below has been compiled with 52 different ways that you can gracefully decline offers without being rude or offensive. It is designed to assist you in this endeavor. Using 52 weeks in a year allows you to explore and practice a new approach each week. Take your time. This is exciting, and the benefits may last a lifetime as long as the outcomes serve you well.

Alternatively, you can select any of the suggestions that deeply resonate with you and gradually incorporate them into your life. Remember, this is a process that requires patience and exploration to determine what works for you. Allow time to develop a pattern. Feel free to adapt and modify the prompts below to align with your unique circumstances and personal preferences. You are always in control.

Be courageous and practice the statements be-low, then reflect on how you felt after using each of them. Be sure to place a checkmark in the box as you try them. Continue to use the ones that work best for you.

Practice Saying No	Week	Tried
Thank you for the offer, but it's not something I can commit to right now.	1	[ ]
I appreciate your consideration, but I have other priorities at the moment.	2	[ ]
I've evaluated my schedule and unfortunately, I won't be able to participate.	3	[ ]
I understand the importance of this opportunity, but I have to decline.	4	[ ]
Thank you for thinking of me, but I'm unable to take it on at this time.	5	[ ]
I value your understanding, but it's not feasible for me to be involved.	6	[ ]
I've carefully considered your request, but I have to respectfully decline.	7	[ ]
I'm grateful for the offer, but it doesn't align with my current focus.	8	[ ]
I appreciate your invitation, but I won't be able to join this time.	9	[ ]
Thank you for including me, but I'm unable to contribute in this capacity.	10	[ ]
I've reflected on your request, but I have to prioritize my own well-being.	11	[ ]

Dr. Katherine Y. Brown

Practice Saying No	Week	Tried
I value our relationship, but I won't be able to accommodate this request.	12	[ ]
I understand the significance of this project, but I'm unable to commit.	13	[ ]
Thank you for your kind offer, but I can't take it on at this time.	14	[ ]
I respect your perspective, but I can't commit to this endeavor.	15	[ ]
I'm sorry, but that doesn't align with my current priorities.	16	[ ]
I've evaluated my workload, and I won't be able to meet this deadline.	17	[ ]
Thank you for reaching out, but I have other commitments that prevent me from participating.	18	[ ]
I value your understanding, but I can't join in at this moment.	19	[ ]
I appreciate your consideration, but I have to decline this invitation.	20	[ ]

Practice Saying No	Week	Tried
I've thought about it, and I'm unable to take on any additional responsibilities.	21	[ ]
I'm sorry, but I won't be able to provide the assistance you are seeking.	22	[ ]
Thank you for thinking of me, but I have to say no this time.	23	[ ]
I appreciate your offer, but it's not something I can commit to.	24	[ ]
I've considered the opportunity, but I can't extend my help at this time.	25	[ ]
I'm grateful for the invitation, but I won't be able to contribute.	26	[ ]
I understand the significance of this task, but I have to prioritize my own goals.	27	[ ]
Thank you for your understanding, but I won't be able to participate.	28	[ ]
I respect your needs, but I'm unable to fulfill this request.	29	[ ]

Dr. Katherine Y. Brown

Practice Saying No	Week	Tried
I appreciate your support, but I can't take on any additional obligations.	30	[ ]
I've evaluated my schedule, and it's not feasible for me to be involved.	31	[ ]
Thank you for your consideration, but I have other commitments that require my attention.	32	[ ]
I value our connection, but I won't be able to accommodate this request.	33	[ ]
I understand the importance of this project, but I have to say *no*.	34	[ ]
I've considered the offer, but I can't commit to it right now.	35	[ ]
I'm sorry, but I won't be able to take on any additional responsibilities.	36	[ ]
I appreciate your consideration, but I can't extend my help at this time.	37	[ ]
I understand the significance of this opportunity, but I have to prioritize my own needs.	38	[ ]

Practice Saying No	Week	Tried
Thank you for thinking of me, but I won't be able to contribute.	39	[ ]
I'm grateful for the opportunity, but I can't commit to it right now.	40	[ ]
I respect your perspective, but I won't be able to join in.	41	[ ]
I appreciate your under-standing, but it's not something I can take on at the moment.	42	[ ]
Thank you for your invita-tion, but I'm unable to participate.	43	[ ]
I'm sorry, but I won't be able to attend.	44	[ ]
I understand the importance of this event, but I won't be able to make it.	45	[ ]
Thank you for your kind offer, but I'm unable to accept it at this time.	46	[ ]
I respect your perspective, but I can't commit to this endeavor.	47	[ ]

Practice Saying No	Week	Tried
I'm sorry, but that doesn't align with my current priorities.	48	[ ]
I've evaluated my work-load, and I won't be able to meet this deadline.	49	[ ]
Thank you for reaching out, but I have other commit-ments that prevent me from participating.	50	[ ]
I value your understanding, but I won't be able to join in at this moment.	51	[ ]
I appreciate your considera-tion, but I have to decline this invitation.	52	[ ]

There are instances when usual solutions may not suffice. In these cases, a clear and direct response is often the most effective approach. For example, a simple "no" without any further explanation can resolve the situation decisively. Embracing the courage to empower yourself by mastering the art of saying no and appreciating how it opens up a world of possibilities. However, be mindful not to fill the newfound time and space with other commitments. Allow yourself the freedom to savor the present moment and nurture your well-being. I wish you continued success and fulfillment on your path of unlocking your "yes" by mastering the "no."

Practicing Ways to Say No

The art of saying no does not come easily to everyone. Many of the ways listed below will seem similar, but that's intentional, reflecting the different ways we express ourselves. Try out some of the examples in the scenarios of ways to say no, then through practice find which one works best for you. Regardless of the setting: work, home, community, etc., you must protect your peace by prioritizing and ensuring that where you invest your time and efforts aligns with what is important to you.

Below, I will reintroduce you to the five tips of the P.E.A.C.E. method: Pause, Evaluate, Assess, Confirm, Embrace. Use them to see a new way to make thoughtful decisions and to say no confidently when necessary. Each scenario will illustrate how you can apply these five tips to different situations in your life. Protect your boundaries using P.E.A.C.E. and always remember to pause, evaluate, assess, confirm, and embrace your decision by using these five tips for P.E.A.C.E.

1. Declining Unnecessary Group Chats

- **Scenario:** You are added to a group chat that

constantly alerts you with irrelevant messages that you find frustrating and disruptive.

- **Pause:** Take a moment to consider how the constant notifications are affecting you.

- **Evaluate:** Think about the impact on your productivity and stress levels.

- **Assess:** Determine if the group chat aligns with your need for focus and calm.

- **Confirm:** Decide that reducing distractions is a priority.

- **Embrace:** Communicate your decision: "I appreciate you adding me, but I'm limiting my group chats." If you want to stay in the group chat you can put the app on silent but you may still be expected to be accountable for checking the notifications.

2. Lending Money to Family

- **Scenario:** Your cousin asks to borrow money, which would require canceling your vacation. You explain this but they insist that they need the money more than you do.

- **Pause:** Reflect on your financial situation and past experiences.

- **Evaluate:** Consider the impact of lending money versus keeping your savings.

- **Assess:** Determine if lending money aligns with your financial priorities.

- **Confirm:** Decide to prioritize your vacation savings.

- **Embrace:** Communicate your decision: "I'm not in a position to lend money right now, but I hope things work out for you."

3. Avoiding Negative Influences

- **Scenario:** You are asked to join a social group that gossips and complains when you have attended their gatherings.

- **Pause:** Reflect on how joining this group

might affect your mindset.

- **Evaluate:** Think about the impact on your mental health and attitude.

- **Assess:** Determine if participating aligns with your values.

- **Confirm:** Decide to maintain a positive environment.

- **Embrace:** Communicate your decision: "Thank you for the invitation but I am unable to attend." If you want to be direct you could say, "I prefer to avoid negative conversations, so I'll pass."

4. Taking Time for Yourself

- **Scenario:** You are invited to multiple social events in one weekend and you do not want to attend them all.

- **Pause:** Reflect on your need for rest and personal time.

- **Evaluate:** Consider the impact of attending all events on your well-being.

- **Assess:** Determine if attending aligns with your need for self-care.

- **Confirm:** Decide to prioritize your rest.

- **Embrace:** Communicate your decision: "I need some time to recharge, so I'll have to pass on all of these events."

5. Not Letting Others' Emergencies Disrupt Your Plans

- **Scenario:** You are asked to help a friend with a non-urgent issue, disrupting your plans that you made for self care. You have recently gone through work challenges, health issues, and some personal family difficulties caring for an ill loved one. This day of self care was a gift to yourself because you have been neglecting your health to care for everyone else.

- **Pause:** Reflect on your current plans and commitments.

- **Evaluate:** Consider the impact of changing your plans. Your natural instinct may be to help the other person which is good however you must evaluate the impact this has on you.

- **Assess:** Determine if helping aligns with your priorities.

- **Confirm:** Decide to stay committed to your original plans.

- **Embrace:** Communicate your decision: "I have preexisting plans that I must prioritize and can't change, but I hope you can manage."

6. Saying No to Unnecessary Activities

- **Scenario:** You are invited on a spontaneous weekend trip you can't afford. Your credit card is overdrawn because you did six unplanned trips with this same group of friends and have overextended yourself. You want to fit in and not be viewed as not having money, but you're working hard to be debt free.

- **Pause:** Reflect on your financial situation.

- **Evaluate:** Consider the impact on your finances and stress levels.

- **Assess:** Determine if this aligns with your financial goals.

- **Confirm:** Decide to prioritize your financial stability.

- **Embrace:** Communicate your decision: "I can't afford a trip right now, but thanks for the invite."

7. Avoiding Over commitment to Community Service

- **Scenario:** You are asked to volunteer for multiple community events in a month. You set a goal of 10 hours of service per month but these requests exceed this and you believe you are overextending yourself.

- **Pause:** Reflect on your current commitments.

- **Evaluate:** Consider the impact on your time and energy.

- **Assess:** Determine if volunteering aligns with your schedule and capacity to volunteer.

- **Confirm:** Decide to maintain balance.

- **Embrace:** Communicate your decision: "I'm committed to other activities, so unfortunately I can't volunteer for all these events."

8. Providing Job Referrals

- **Scenario:** A colleague asks for a job referral but you do not believe you can give a positive evaluation. You also have limited time to complete it, although your major concern is that you do not want to recommend them.

- **Pause:** Reflect on your experience with the colleague.

- **Evaluate:** Consider the potential impact on your reputation.

- **Assess:** Determine if providing a referral aligns with your professional integrity.

- **Confirm:** Decide to protect your professional standing.

- **Embrace:** Communicate your decision: "I don't feel comfortable providing a referral at this time."

9. **Taking on a Leadership Role**

- **Scenario:** You are asked to take on a leadership role for a new project. You're intrigued by the project but find that taking on a leadership role increases your stress and makes the project not enjoyable.

- **Pause:** Reflect on your current workload.

- **Evaluate:** Consider the impact on your stress levels and performance.

- **Assess:** Determine if taking on the role aligns with your capacity.

- **Confirm:** Decide to prioritize your well-being.

- **Embrace:** Communicate your decision: "I'm flattered, but I can't take on a leadership role right now. Can I support the project in another way?"

10. Paying for Too Many Organization Membership Dues

- **Scenario:** You are asked to renew multiple professional organization memberships. You have decided that you need to reduce the memberships.

- **Pause:** Reflect on your budget.

- **Evaluate:** Consider the impact on your finances.

- **Assess:** Determine which membership renewals align with your financial priorities.

- **Confirm:** Decide to prioritize your budget.

- **Embrace:** Communicate your decision: "I'm prioritizing my memberships and won't be renewing this one."

11. Declining a Loan to a Friend

- **Scenario:** A friend asks to borrow a large sum of money.

- **Pause:** Reflect on your financial situation.

- **Evaluate:** Consider the impact on your finances and relationship.

- **Assess:** Determine if lending aligns with your financial goals.

- **Confirm:** Decide to protect your financial stability.

- **Embrace:** Communicate your decision: "I'm not in a position to lend money right now."

12. Making Time for Exercise

- **Scenario:** You are asked to help a friend move into their apartment on your scheduled workout day.

- **Pause:** Reflect on your fitness goals.

- **Evaluate:** Consider the impact on your health.

- **Assess:** Determine if helping aligns with your priorities.

- **Confirm:** Decide to prioritize your workout.

- **Embrace:** Communicate your decision: "I have a workout scheduled, but I can help another day."

13. Avoiding Unnecessary Spending

- **Scenario:** You are invited to a shopping spree with friends.

- **Pause:** Reflect on your budget.

- **Evaluate:** Consider the impact on your finances.

- **Assess:** Determine if shopping aligns with your financial goals.

- **Confirm:** Decide to prioritize saving money.

- **Embrace:** Communicate your decision: "I'm saving money right now, so I'll have to pass."

14. Procrastination On Your Plans Due to Helping Others

- **Scenario:** You are asked to help a colleague with their project while you have your own deadlines.

- **Pause:** Reflect on your deadlines.

- **Evaluate:** Consider the impact on your work.

- **Assess:** Determine if helping aligns with your priorities.

- **Confirm:** Decide to prioritize your tasks.

- **Embrace:** Communicate your decision: "I need to focus on my existing deadlines and won't be able to assist."

15. Saying No with Without An Explanation Needed

- **Scenario:** You are asked to do something that compromises your ethics and integrity.

- **Pause:** Reflect on the request and how it conflicts with your values.

- **Evaluate:** Consider the impact on your personal integrity and professional reputation.

- **Assess:** Determine if this aligns with your principles and ethical standards.

- **Confirm:** Decide to uphold your ethics and integrity.

- **Embrace:** Communicate your decision: "No."

Your yes and your no will always cost you something. When you say yes to one thing, you are inherently saying no to something else. This is why it's critical to consider the return on investment (ROI) of your time and life decisions. Time is a resource; once spent, it can never be reclaimed. Just like financial investments, where opportunity cost represents the potential gain lost when choosing one alternative over another, your decisions about where to invest your time and efforts also come with opportunity costs.

Saying yes to obligations that do not align with your values or priorities can lead to stress, burnout, and missed opportunities for personal growth and happiness. For instance, agreeing to an extra project at work might mean losing valuable time with your family or missing out on self-care activities. When you weigh the cost of your yes against the benefits it brings, you can make more informed and intentional choices. By learning to say no effectively, you protect your peace and ensure that your time and energy are invested in what truly matters to you. Remember, saying no is not about rejecting others; it's about affirming your own priorities and well-being.

Use the scenarios and strategies outlined above to continue practicing saying no confidently and respectfully, and you may quickly observe that your life becomes more aligned with your values and goals.

This is only the beginning. The best is yet to come. Be patient, trust your process, and take it one day at a time. Congratulations in advance on choosing YOU!

Join the I Am Amazing Movement!

The KYB Leadership Academy mission is to empower 1 million youth around the globe. Your tax-deductible sponsorship will help our future leaders discover how truly AMAZING they are! Scan the QR code to choose a sponsorship level!

Scan to Pay

Books By Dr. Katherine Y. Brown

Embrace Your No: Five Tips To Unlock Your Life and Find Peace.

I Am Authentic: 103 Tips For Becoming Your True Self

Imbalance: The Perception of Unfulfillment of The Modern Day Woman

I Am Courageous: Empowering Quotes for Courageous and Optimistic Living

Never Forget You: A Five-Step Guide To Self-Care

A Letter To Myself: Three Steps to Confronting Fear, Embracing Failure, and Celebrating Success

Journal: Journey of Optimism, Understanding, Reflection, Nurturing, Acceptance, and Love

I Am Amazing

www.ingramcontent.com/pod-product-compliance
Lightning Source LLC
Chambersburg PA
CBHW071154120626
46546CB00006B/2264